NON-ALCOHOLIC COCKTAILS

COPYRIGHT

unique needs and this book cannot take these individual differences in account.

1. LEMON-BASIL MOJITO MOCKTAILS

Ingredients

1-1/2 cups sugar

4 cups water

6 cups fresh basil leaves, divided

Crushed ice, divided

2 bottles (1 liter each) club soda

GARNISH:

Fresh lemon wedges

Directions

In a small saucepan, bring sugar and water to a boil. Cook and stir until sugar is dissolved. Place half of the basil in a small bowl. With a pestle or wooden spoon, crush basil until its aroma is released. Stir into sugar mixture. Remove from heat; cool completely. Strain; refrigerate until cold.

Place 2 cups crushed ice and remaining basil in a 4-qt. pitcher. Using a muddler or a wooden spoon, press basil leaves against ice until their aroma is released. Stir in basil syrup and soda. Serve over crushed ice in tall glasses; squeeze lemon wedges into drink.

Total Time

Prep: 15 min. + chilling

Makes

12 servings

Nutrition Facts

1 serving: 101 calories, 0 fat (0 saturated fat), 0 cholesterol, 36mg sodium, 26g carbohydrate (25g sugars, 0 fiber), 0 protein.

2. RASPBERRY FIZZ

Ingredients

2 ounces ruby red grapefruit juice

1/2 to 1 ounce raspberry flavoring syrup

1/2 to 3/4 cup ice cubes

6 ounces club soda, chilled

Directions

In a mixing glass or tumbler, combine grapefruit juice and syrup. Place ice in a highball glass; add juice mixture. Top with club soda.

Total Time

Prep/Total Time: 5 min.

Makes

1 serving

Nutrition Facts

1 each: 70 calories, 0 fat (0 saturated fat), 0 cholesterol, 37mg sodium, 18g carbohydrate (12g sugars, 0 fiber), 0 protein. Diabetic Exchanges: 1 starch.

3. ICED MELON MOROCCAN MINT TEA

Ingredients

2 cups water

12 fresh mint leaves

4 individual green tea bags

1/3 cup sugar

2-1/2 cups diced honeydew melon

1-1/2 cups ice cubes

Additional ice cubes

Directions

In a large saucepan, bring water to a boil. Remove from the heat; add mint and tea bags. Cover and steep for 3-5 minutes. Discard mint and tea bags. Stir in the sugar.

In a blender, process honeydew until blended. Add 1-1/2 cups ice and tea; process until blended. Serve over additional ice.

Total Time

Prep/Total Time: 20 min.

Makes

5 servings

Nutrition Facts

1 cup: 81 calories, 0 fat (0 saturated fat), 0 cholesterol, 9mg sodium, 21g carbohydrate (21g sugars, 1g fiber), 0 protein. Diabetic Exchanges: 1 starch.

4. CRANBERRY LIMEADE

Ingredients

2-1/2 to 3-1/2 cups water, divided

1-1/4 cups sugar

2 to 3 cups cranberry juice

1-1/2 cups lime juice (10 to 12 medium limes)

1 tablespoon grated lime zest

Ice cubes

Lime slices, optional

Directions

Bring 1-1/2 cups water and sugar to a boil. Remove from heat; stir in juices, lime zest and remaining water. Cover; refrigerate at least 1 hour. Serve over ice and, if desired, with lime slices.

Total Time

Prep: 15 min. + chilling

Makes

7 servings

Nutrition Facts

1 cup: 186 calories, 0 fat (0 saturated fat), 0 cholesterol, 3mg sodium, 49g carbohydrate (46g sugars, 0 fiber), 1g protein.

5. BLACKBERRY SHRUB

Ingredients

1-1/2 cups fresh or frozen blackberries, crushed

1 cinnamon stick (about 3 inches)

1 cup cider vinegar

1-1/2 cups sugar

1/2 cup water

SERVING SUGGESTION:

Ice cubes, sparkling water and fresh blackberries, optional

Directions

Place fruit and cinnamon stick in a sterilized pint jar. Bring vinegar just to a boil; pour over fruit, leaving ¼-in. headspace. Center lid on jar; screw on band until fingertip tight. Refrigerate for 1 week.

Strain vinegar mixture through a fine-mesh strainer into another sterilized pint jar. Press solids to extract juice; discard remaining fruit.

Bring sugar and water to a boil. Reduce heat; simmer until sugar is dissolved. Cool slightly. Stir into vinegar mixture; shake well. Store in the refrigerator up to 2 weeks.

To serve, drink 1-2 tablespoons or add to a glass of ice, top with sparkling water and garnish with fresh blackberries.

Total Time

Prep: 10 min. Cook: 20 min + chilling

Makes

2 cups

Nutrition Facts

2 tablespoons blackberry shrub syrup: 83 calories, 0 fat (0 saturated fat), 0 cholesterol, 1mg sodium, 20g carbohydrate (20g sugars, 1g fiber), 0 protein.

6. ROSEMARY LEMONADE

Ingredients

2 cups water

2 fresh rosemary sprigs

1/2 cup sugar

1/2 cup honey

1-1/4 cups fresh lemon juice

6 cups cold water

Ice cubes

Additional lemon slices and fresh rosemary sprigs, optional

Directions

In a small saucepan, bring 2 cups water to a boil; add rosemary sprigs. Reduce heat; simmer, covered, 10 minutes.

Remove and discard rosemary. Stir in sugar and honey until dissolved. Transfer to a pitcher; refrigerate 15 minutes.

Add lemon juice; stir in cold water. Serve over ice. If desired, top with additional lemon slices and rosemary sprigs.

Total Time

Prep: 10 min. Cook: 15 min. + chilling

Makes

8 servings (1 cup each)

Nutrition Facts

1 cup: 121 calories, 0 fat (0 saturated fat), 0 cholesterol, 1mg sodium, 33g carbohydrate (31g sugars, 0 fiber), 0 protein.

7. WATERMELON-LIME COOLER

Ingredients

12 cups cubed seedless watermelon, frozen, divided

3/4 teaspoon grated lime zest, divided

6 cups chilled ginger ale, divided

Directions

Place 4 cups frozen watermelon, 1/4 teaspoon lime zest and 2 cups ginger ale in a blender; cover and process until slushy. Serve immediately. Repeat twice.

Total Time

Prep/Total Time: 10 min.

Makes

12 servings

Nutrition Facts

1 cup: 82 calories, 0 fat (0 saturated fat), 0 cholesterol, 14mg sodium, 24g carbohydrate (23g sugars, 1g fiber), 1g protein.

8. STRAWBERRY-BASIL REFRESHER

Ingredients

2/3 cup lemon juice

1/2 cup sugar

1 cup sliced fresh strawberries

Ice cubes

1 to 2 tablespoons chopped fresh basil

1 bottle (1 liter) club soda, chilled

Directions

Place lemon juice, sugar, strawberries and 1 cup ice cubes in a blender; cover and process until blended. Add basil; pulse 1 or 2 times to combine.

Divide strawberry mixture among 12 cocktail glasses. Fill with ice; top with club soda.

Total Time

Prep/Total Time: 10 min.

Makes

12 servings

Nutrition Facts

1 serving: 40 calories, 0 fat (0 saturated fat), 0 cholesterol, 18mg sodium, 10g carbohydrate (9g sugars, 0 fiber), 0 protein. Diabetic Exchanges: 1/2 starch.

9. ICED HONEYDEW MINT TEA

Ingredients

4 cups water

24 fresh mint leaves

8 green tea bags

2/3 cup sugar

5 cups diced honeydew melon

3 cups ice cubes

Additional ice cubes

Directions

In a large saucepan, bring water to a boil; remove from heat. Add mint leaves and tea bags; steep, covered, 3-5 minutes according to taste, stirring occasionally. Discard mint and tea bags. Stir in sugar.

Place 2-1/2 cups honeydew, 2 cups tea and 1-1/2 cups ice in a blender; cover and process until blended. Serve over additional ice. Repeat with remaining ingredients.

Total Time

Prep/Total Time: 20 min.

Makes

10 servings

Nutrition Facts

1 cup: 83 calories, 0 fat (0 saturated fat), 0 cholesterol, 15mg sodium, 21g carbohydrate (20g sugars, 1g fiber), 0 protein. Diabetic Exchanges: 1 starch, 1/2 fruit.

10. WATERMELON-STRAWBERRY COOLER

Ingredients

2 cups water

1/2 cup lemon juice

12 cups cubed watermelon (about 3-1/2 pounds)

2 cups fresh strawberries or raspberries

2/3 cup sugar

1-1/2 teaspoons minced fresh mint

Small watermelon wedges and fresh mint leaves

Directions

Place 1 cup water, 1/4 cup lemon juice, 6 cups watermelon, 1 cup berries, 1/3 cup sugar and 3/4 teaspoon minced mint in a blender; cover and process until smooth. Transfer to a large pitcher. Repeat with remaining water, lemon juice, fruit, sugar and minced mint.

Refrigerate 1 hour or until cold. If desired, press through a fine-mesh strainer. Serve with watermelon wedges and mint leaves.

Total Time

Prep: 10 min. + chilling

Makes

10 servings (1 cup each)

Nutrition Facts

1 cup: 119 calories, 0 fat (0 saturated fat), 0 cholesterol, 2mg sodium, 30g carbohydrate (26g sugars, 1g fiber), 1g protein.

11. RHUBARB MINT TEA

Ingredients

4 cups chopped fresh or frozen rhubarb

2 cups fresh or frozen raspberries

2 packages (3/4 ounce each) fresh mint leaves

3 quarts water

4 black tea bags

2 cups sugar

12 mint sprigs

Directions

In a 6-qt. stockpot, combine rhubarb, raspberries, mint and water; bring to a boil. Reduce heat; simmer, uncovered, 30 minutes. Remove from heat. Add tea bags; steep, covered, 3-5 minutes according to taste. Using a fine mesh strainer, strain tea, discarding tea bags and pulp. Stir in sugar until dissolved; cool slightly. Transfer to a pitcher; refrigerate until cooled completely. Serve over ice with mint sprigs.

Total Time

Prep: 15 min. Cook: 45 min. + chilling

Makes

12 servings (1 cup each)

Nutrition Facts

1 cup: 151 calories, 0 fat (0 saturated fat), 0 cholesterol, 3mg sodium, 38g carbohydrate (35g sugars, 2g fiber), 1g protein.

12. GRILLED LEMON & THYME LEMONADE

Ingredients

15 fresh thyme sprigs

2 cups water, divided

1 cup sugar, divided

9 medium lemons, halved

1/4 cup honey

1/4 teaspoon almond extract

5 cups cold water

Directions

In a small bowl, soak thyme sprigs in 1 cup water while preparing lemons. Place 1/4 cup sugar on a plate; dip cut sides of lemons in sugar.

Cover and grill lemons, cut side down, over medium-high heat for 1-2 minutes or until golden brown. Cool slightly. Drain thyme; grill for 1-2 minutes or until lightly browned, turning once.

In a small saucepan, combine 1 cup water, honey and remaining sugar; bring to a boil, stirring constantly to dissolve sugar. Remove from the heat. Add grilled thyme sprigs and extract; let stand for 1 hour to steep. Discard thyme.

Meanwhile, squeeze lemons to obtain 1-1/2 cups juice; strain. In a large pitcher, combine 5 cups cold water, thyme syrup and lemon juice. Serve over ice.

Total Time

Prep: 25 min. + standing Cook: 5 min.

Makes

9 servings (1 cup each)

13. PRETTY PINK PUNCH

Ingredients

2 tablespoons sugar

3 cups cold water

2 bottles (64 ounces each) cranberry-raspberry juice, chilled

1 can (46 ounces) pineapple juice, chilled

1 can (12 ounces) frozen pink lemonade concentrate, thawed

1 liter ginger ale, chilled

Decorative ice mold & lemon slices, optional

Directions

In a punch bowl, dissolve sugar in water. Add juices and lemonade; mix well. Stir in ginger ale. If desired, top with a decorative ice mold and lemon slices. Serve immediately.

Total Time

Prep/Total Time: 15 min.

Makes

50 servings (7-1/2 quarts)

Nutrition Facts

1/2 cup: 76 calories, 0 fat (0 saturated fat), 0 cholesterol, 5mg sodium, 19g carbohydrate (18g sugars, 0 fiber), 0 protein.

14. BANANA BRUNCH PUNCH

Ingredients

6 medium ripe bananas

1 can (12 ounces) frozen orange juice concentrate, thawed

3/4 cup thawed lemonade concentrate

3 cups warm water, divided

2 cups sugar, divided

1 can (46 ounces) pineapple juice, chilled

3 bottles (2 liters each) lemon-lime soda, chilled

Orange slices, optional

Directions

In a blender, cover and process the bananas, orange juice and lemonade until smooth. Remove half of the mixture and set aside. Add 1-1/2 cups warm water and 1 cup sugar to blender; blend until smooth.

Place in a large freezer container. Repeat with remaining banana mixture, water and sugar; add to container. Cover and freeze until solid.

One hour before serving, remove punch base from freezer. Just before serving, place in a large punch bowl. Add pineapple juice and soda; stir until well blended. Garnish with orange slices if desired.

Total Time

Prep: 10 min. + freezing

Makes

60-70 servings (10 quarts)

Nutrition Facts

3/4 cup: 68 calories, 0 fat (0 saturated fat), 0 cholesterol, 4mg sodium, 17g carbohydrate (16g sugars, 0 fiber), 0 protein.

15. VIRGIN HURRICANES

Ingredients

2 cups passion fruit juice

1 cup unsweetened pineapple juice

1 cup orange juice

3/4 cup lemon juice

2 cups carbonated water

Ice cubes

Pineapple wedges and maraschino cherries

Directions

Combine the juices in a pitcher. Just before serving, stir in carbonated water. Pour into hurricane or highball glasses filled with ice. Garnish with pineapple wedges and cherries.

Total Time

Prep/Total Time: 10 min.

Makes

9 servings (3/4 cup each)

Nutrition Facts

3/4 cup (calculated without garnishes): 61 calories, 0 fat (0 saturated fat), 0 cholesterol, 6mg sodium, 15g carbohydrate (12g sugars, 0 fiber), 0 protein. Diabetic Exchanges: 1 fruit.

16. ORANGE LEMONADE

Ingredients

1-3/4 cups sugar

2-1/2 cups water

2 tablespoons grated lemon zest

2 tablespoons grated orange zest

1-1/2 cups lemon juice (about 10 lemons)

1-1/2 cups orange juice (about 5 oranges)

6 cups cold water

Directions

In a large saucepan, combine sugar and 2-1/2 cups water; cook and stir over medium heat until sugar is dissolved. Cool slightly.

Stir in citrus zest and juices. Let stand, covered, 1 hour. Strain syrup; refrigerate, covered, until cold.

To serve, fill glasses or pitcher with an equal amount of fruit syrup and water. Add ice and serve.

Total Time

Prep: 15 min. + chilling Cook: 5 min. + cooling

Makes

12 servings

Nutrition Facts

1 cup: 136 calories, 0 fat (0 saturated fat), 0 cholesterol, 1mg sodium, 35g carbohydrate (33g sugars, 0 fiber), 0 protein.

17. SENSATIONAL SLUSH

Ingredients

1/2 cup sugar

1 package (3 ounces) strawberry gelatin

2 cups boiling water

1 cup unsweetened pineapple juice

2 cups sliced fresh strawberries

1 can (12 ounces) frozen lemonade concentrate, thawed

1 can (12 ounces) frozen limeade concentrate, thawed

2 cups cold water

2 liters lemon-lime soda, chilled

Directions

In a large bowl, dissolve sugar and gelatin in boiling water. In a blender, combine pineapple juice and strawberries; cover and process until blended. Add to gelatin mixture. Stir in concentrates and cold water. Cover and freeze for 8 hours or overnight.

Remove from the freezer 45 minutes before serving. For each serving, combine 1/2 cup slush mixture with 1/2 cup lemon-lime soda; stir well.

Total Time

Prep: 25 min. + freezing

Makes

20 servings

Nutrition Facts

1 cup: 151 calories, 0 fat (0 saturated fat), 0 cholesterol, 22mg sodium, 39g carbohydrate (35g sugars, 1g fiber), 1g protein.

18. LEMON-LIME PUNCH

Ingredients

2 quarts water

2 cups sugar

2 envelopes unsweetened lemon-lime soft drink mix

1 can (46 ounces) unsweetened pineapple juice

1 liter ginger ale, chilled

1 quart lime sherbet

Directions

In a punch bowl, combine the water, sugar and soft drink mix; stir until dissolved. Stir in pineapple juice. Refrigerate until chilled. Just before serving, stir in ginger ale and top with scoops of sherbet.

Total Time

Prep: 10 min. + chilling

Makes

6 quarts

Nutrition Facts

1 cup: 146 calories, 1g fat (0 saturated fat), 0 cholesterol, 19mg sodium, 36g carbohydrate (32g sugars, 1g fiber), 0 protein.

19. PINK RHUBARB PUNCH

Ingredients

8 cups chopped fresh or frozen rhubarb

8 cups water

2-1/2 cups sugar

2 tablespoons strawberry gelatin powder

2 cups boiling water

2 cups pineapple juice

1/4 cup lemon juice

6 cups ginger ale, chilled

Fresh pineapple wedges, sliced strawberries and sliced lemons, optional

Directions

In a Dutch oven, bring rhubarb and water to a boil. Reduce heat; simmer, uncovered, for 10 minutes. Drain, reserving liquid (save rhubarb for another use).

In a large bowl, dissolve sugar and gelatin powder in boiling water. Stir in pineapple and lemon juices. Stir in rhubarb liquid; refrigerate until chilled.

Just before serving, pour into a punch bowl and stir in ginger ale. If desired, garnish with fruit.

Total Time

Prep: 30 min. + chilling

Makes

about 5 quarts

Nutrition Facts

1 cup: 152 calories, 0 fat (0 saturated fat), 0 cholesterol, 11mg sodium, 38g carbohydrate (37g sugars, 1g fiber), 1g protein.

20. RASPBERRY LEMONADE CONCENTRATE

Ingredients

4 pounds fresh raspberries (about 14 cups)

6 cups sugar

4 cups lemon juice

Chilled tonic water or ginger ale

Ice cubes

Directions

Place raspberries in a food processor; cover and process until blended. Strain raspberries, reserving juice. Discard seeds. Place juice in a Dutch oven; stir in sugar and lemon juice. Heat over medium-high heat to 190°. Do not boil.

Remove from heat; skim off foam. Carefully ladle hot mixture into five hot 1-pint jars, leaving 1/4-in. headspace. Wipe rims; screw on bands until fingertip tight.

Place jars into canner simmering water, ensuring that they are completely covered with water. Bring to a boil; process for 10 minutes. Remove jars and cool.

To use concentrate: Mix 1 pint concentrate with 1 pint tonic water. Serve over ice.

Total Time

Prep: 30 min. Process: 10 min.

Makes

5 pints of concentrate (4 servings each)

Nutrition Facts

1 cup: 319 calories, 0 fat (0 saturated fat), 0 cholesterol, 20mg sodium, 83g carbohydrate (78g sugars, 1g fiber), 1g protein.

Printed in Great Britain
by Amazon

77544254R00031